FRANCIS FRITH'S

NANTWICH AND CREWE

PHOTOGRAPHIC MEMORIES

DOROTHY NICOLLE was born in Uganda and later lived in Hong Kong. She was educated in Belfast and at Leicester University where she attained a degree in British Archaeology and History. She has also lived in the Middle East and in France. This gypsy life has encouraged a love of Britain and its history so that, these days, she knows that she has the perfect job - she is a Blue Badge Guide. She also lectures on various aspects of local and general history. Dorothy is married and now lives in Shropshire where she and her husband enjoy walking in the hills with their dogs.

FRANCIS FRITH'S
PHOTOGRAPHIC MEMORIES

NANTWICH
AND CREWE

PHOTOGRAPHIC MEMORIES

DOROTHY NICOLLE

First published in the United Kingdom in 2004 by
Frith Book Company Ltd

Paperback Edition 2004
ISBN 1-85937-648-7

British Library Cataloguing in Publication Data

Francis Frith's Nantwich and Crewe Photographic Memories
Dorothy Nicolle
ISBN 1-85937-648-7

Frith Book Company Ltd
Frith's Barn, Teffont,
Salisbury, Wiltshire SP3 5QP
Tel: +44 (0) 1722 716 376
Email: info@francisfrith.co.uk
www.francisfrith.co.uk

Printed and bound in Great Britain

Front Cover: **NANTWICH** *High Street c1965* N3065
Frontispiece: **CREWE** *Market Street c1955* C316032

*The colour-tinting is for illustrative purposes only, and is not intended to
be historically accurate*

AS WITH ANY HISTORICAL DATABASE THE FRITH ARCHIVE IS CONSTANTLY
BEING CORRECTED AND IMPROVED AND THE PUBLISHERS WOULD
WELCOME INFORMATION ON OMISSIONS OR INACCURACIES

CONTENTS

FRANCIS FRITH
VICTORIAN PIONEER

FRANCIS FRITH, founder of the world-famous photographic archive, was a complex and multi-talented man. A devout Quaker and a highly successful Victorian businessman, he was philosophical by nature and pioneering in outlook.

By 1855 he had already established a wholesale grocery business in Liverpool, and sold it for the astonishing sum of £200,000, which is the equivalent today of over £15,000,000. Now a very rich man, he was able to indulge his passion for travel. As a child he had pored over travel books written by early explorers, and his fancy and imagination had been stirred by family holidays to the sublime mountain regions of Wales and Scotland. 'What lands of spirit-stirring and enriching scenes and places!' he had written. He was to return to these scenes of grandeur in later years to 'recapture the thousands of vivid and tender memories', but with a different purpose. Now in his thirties, and captivated by the new science of photography, Frith set out on a series of pioneering journeys up the Nile and to the Near East that occupied him from 1856 until 1860.

INTRIGUE AND EXPLORATION

These far-flung journeys were packed with intrigue and adventure. In his life story, written when he was sixty-three, Frith tells of being held captive by bandits, and of fighting 'an awful midnight battle to the very point of surrender with a deadly pack of hungry, wild dogs'. Wearing flowing Arab costume, Frith arrived at Akaba by camel sixty years before Lawrence of Arabia, where he encountered 'desert princes and rival sheikhs, blazing with jewel-hilted swords'.

He was the first photographer to venture beyond the sixth cataract of the Nile. Africa was still the mysterious 'Dark Continent', and Stanley and Livingstone's historic meeting was a decade into the future. The conditions for picture taking confound belief. He laboured for hours in his wicker dark-room in the sweltering heat of the desert, while the volatile chemicals fizzed dangerously in their trays. Back in London he exhibited his photographs and was 'rapturously cheered' by members of the Royal Society. His reputation as a photographer was made overnight.

VENTURE OF A LIFE-TIME

Characteristically, Frith quickly spotted the opportunity to create a new business as a specialist publisher of photographs. He lived in an era of immense and sometimes violent change.

For the poor in the early part of Victoria's reign work was exhausting and the hours long, and people had precious little free time to enjoy themselves. Most had no transport other than a cart or gig at their disposal, and rarely travelled far beyond the boundaries of their own town or village. However, by the 1870s the railways had threaded their way across the country, and Bank Holidays and half-day Saturdays had been made obligatory by Act of Parliament. All of a sudden the working man and his family were able to enjoy days out and see a little more of the world.

With typical business acumen, Francis Frith foresaw that these new tourists would enjoy having souvenirs to commemorate their days out. In 1860 he married Mary Ann Rosling and set out on a new career: his aim was to photograph every city, town and village in Britain. For the next thirty years he travelled the country by train and by pony and trap, producing fine photographs of seaside resorts and beauty spots that were keenly bought by millions of Victorians. These prints were painstakingly pasted into family albums and pored over during the dark nights of winter, rekindling precious memories of summer excursions.

THE RISE OF FRITH & CO

Frith's studio was soon supplying retail shops all over the country. To meet the demand he gathered about him a small team of photographers, and published the work of independent artist-photographers of the calibre of Roger Fenton and Francis Bedford. In order to gain some understanding of the scale of Frith's business one only has to look at the catalogue issued by Frith & Co in 1886: it runs to some 670 pages, listing not only many thousands of views of the British Isles but also many photographs of most European countries, and China, Japan, the USA and Canada - note the sample page shown on page 9 from the hand-written Frith & Co ledgers recording the pictures. By 1890 Frith had created the greatest specialist photographic publishing company in the world, with over 2,000 sales outlets - more than the combined number that Boots and WH Smith have today! The picture on the next page shows the Frith & Co display board at Ingleton in the Yorkshire Dales (left of window). Beautifully constructed with a mahogany frame and gilt inserts, it could display up to a dozen local scenes.

POSTCARD BONANZA

The ever-popular holiday postcard we know today took many years to develop. In 1870 the Post Office issued the first plain cards, with a pre-printed stamp on one face. In 1894 they allowed other publishers' cards to be sent through the mail with an attached adhesive halfpenny stamp. Demand grew rapidly, and in 1895 a new size of postcard was permitted called the court card, but there was little room for illustration. In 1899, a year after Frith's death, a new card measuring 5.5 x 3.5 inches became the standard format, but it was not until 1902 that the divided back came into being, so that the address and message could be on one face and a full-size illustration on the other. Frith & Co were in the vanguard of postcard development: Frith's sons Eustace and Cyril continued their father's monumental task, expanding the number of views offered to the public and recording more and more places in Britain, as the

coasts and countryside were opened up to mass travel.

Francis Frith had died in 1898 at his villa in Cannes, his great project still growing. The archive he created continued in business for another seventy years. By 1970 it contained over a third of a million pictures showing 7,000 British towns and villages.

FRANCIS FRITH'S LEGACY

Frith's legacy to us today is of immense significance and value, for the magnificent archive of evocative photographs he created provides a unique record of change in the cities, towns and villages throughout Britain over a century and more. Frith and his fellow studio photographers revisited locations many times down the years to update their views, compiling for us an enthralling and colourful pageant of British life and character.

We are fortunate that Frith was dedicated to recording the minutiae of everyday life. For it is this sheer wealth of visual data, the painstaking chronicle of changes in dress, transport, street layouts, buildings, housing, engineering and landscape that captivates us so much today. His remarkable images offer us a powerful link with the past and with the lives of our ancestors.

THE VALUE OF THE ARCHIVE TODAY

Computers have now made it possible for Frith's many thousands of images to be accessed almost instantly. Frith's images are increasingly used as visual resources, by social historians, by researchers into genealogy and ancestry, by architects and town planners, and by teachers involved in local history projects.

In addition, the archive offers every one of us an opportunity to examine the places where we and our families have lived and worked down the years. Highly successful in Frith's own era, the archive is now, a century and more on, entering a new phase of popularity. Historians consider the Francis Frith Collection to be of prime national importance. It is the only archive of its kind remaining in private ownership. Francis Frith's archive is now housed in an historic timber barn in the beautiful village of Teffont in Wiltshire. Its founder would not recognize the archive office as it is today. In place of the many thousands of dusty boxes containing glass plate negatives and an all-pervading odour of photographic chemicals, there are now ranks of computer screens. He would be amazed to watch his images travelling round the world at unimaginable speeds through internet lines.

The archive's future is both bright and exciting. Francis Frith, with his unshakeable belief in making photographs available to the greatest number of people, would undoubtedly approve of what is being done today with his lifetime's work. His photographs depicting our shared past are now bringing pleasure and enlightenment to millions around the world a century and more after his death.

THE PARISH CHURCH *1898* 42190

Having survived the great fire of 1583, St Mary's Church
is the oldest building in the town. Much of the structure
dates from the 14th century, although it is thought that
building work was probably interrupted by the Black
Death and only resumed much later that same century.

THE PARISH CHURCH *1898* 42187

This stunningly beautiful church is known as the 'cathedral of south Cheshire'. In fact, it is the only church in Cheshire that Simon Jenkins in his recent book *England's Thousand Best Churches* placed in his top one hundred. Yet until the 16th century it was just a chapel of ease for nearby Acton church, which was considered to be far more important.

NANTWICH

OF THE TWO TOWNS of Nantwich and Crewe, Nantwich is the one whose antecedents go back to the beginnings of our history. The salt pits here were probably first worked by the Romans, if not earlier. Certainly salt ('sal' in Latin) was such an important commodity to the Romans that they often paid their soldiers with it – hence our word 'salary' today.

It is possible that after the Romans left our shores, the Welsh may well have developed the salt works. Their name for this settlement was 'Hellath-wen', meaning 'the white brine pit'. It is fitting that this name still survives today in a street in a modern housing estate.

But it was the Saxons who really developed the salt industry here, and gave the town the name that we know it by. The word 'wich' was an old Saxon word meaning 'the salt works'; the word 'nant' meant 'named' or 'renowned'. In other words, this was one of the most important sources of salt in the country. By the time the Normans invaded in 1066, there were numerous salt pits being worked here. But as the Normans rode roughshod over the country, they provoked a number of uprisings, and there appears to have been a battle here around 1069; the end result was that only one pit was left in production. This was the salt spring later to be known as Old Biot, and it was used right up to the 19th century before it was finally abandoned. It produced more salt than all the other pits in Cheshire added together. Today, this spring still provides brine - it is used (diluted) for an outdoor swimming pool.

Salt was vital for the preservation of food in the days before refrigeration, so this town, as the source of salt, was of considerable importance. This may go some way to explaining why, when in 1583 the town suffered a severe fire, Queen Elizabeth was so ready to donate money of her own and to encourage a nationwide fund-raising appeal for its rebuilding. With so many timber structures in all our towns and villages, fire was a constant threat at this time; certainly, such a national fund-raising appeal was by no means the norm.

That particular fire was a real disaster – it raged for fifteen hours and almost totally destroyed the town. It is said to have caused damage costing £30,000, which was a phenomenal amount of money in those times. Apparently the fire-fighters were not helped in their efforts by the landlord of the Bear Inn, who kept his own bears on the premises for the amusement of his customers. In order to save them, he released the bears as the fire took hold, and the terrified animals must have caused total mayhem amongst the no less terrified townspeople.

Having recovered from the fire, the town was then to suffer in the 1600s during the Civil War. In a county that began the war generally supporting the Royalist cause, the people of Nantwich went the other way and supported Parliament (one townsman, Thomas Harrison, was an MP and a future signatory of Charles I's death warrant). Consequently, the town was soon captured by the Royalists. It was then retaken by Parliament, who based their garrison here;

it is therefore hardly surprising that it was soon besieged once more by the Royalists, who set up their camp at nearby Dorfold Hall.

This siege lasted for a period of six weeks until 25 January 1644, when the town was relieved by a force of Parliamentarians in what has since been known as the Battle of Nantwich. Ever afterwards, on the Saturday closest to 25 January each year (which is now known as Holly Holy Day), the local people wear a sprig of holly in their hats to commemorate that victory.

Nantwich served also as an important local market town, so it may seem surprising that when the first railway line was suggested nearly 200 years ago, there was a deliberate choice on the part of the people of Nantwich that it should not come through their town. They had just constructed a new canal, and the townsfolk (especially the canal owners) did not want any competition. This means that today Nantwich is considerably smaller than Crewe; but perhaps it is thanks to this decision that so much of the early history of the town survives in the form of its church and some of the delightful buildings that can be found here.

Of course, the railway did eventually come through Nantwich - but only as a branch line. Then the canal owners' fears were indeed realised when local goods were transported by rail instead of canal – this included thousands of gallons of milk from surrounding farms that was sent to supply the industrial towns of nearby Lancashire.

Despite its subsequent decline the canal is now once again in regular use, this time serving the many holidaymakers who discover, when they reach Nantwich, a most delightful and attractive small town.

THE PARISH CHURCH
From the South East 1898 42189

This view shows the fine octagonal crossing tower enclosing the old belfry. The church was (some say excessively!) restored in 1855-79 by Sir George Gilbert Scott, and below the tower there is today a particularly fine crossing vault to his design.

THE PARISH CHURCH, *The Nave Looking East 1898* 42191

Following the dissolution of the monasteries in the 1500s, this became the parish church for the town. In the early 1660s the floor of the church was raised 18 inches to lift it above flood level – there is a window in the floor of the nave where the old floor level can be seen. During the Civil War, the church was used to hold prisoners captured at the Battle of Nantwich.

THE PARISH CHURCH, *The Choir 1898* 42192

This photograph, looking west from the altar, gives a good
impression of one of the glories of Nantwich's church – the
wonderful carving detail in the choir. The choir canopies are
quite simply superb. But the misericords are especially delightful,
with exotic animals, a mermaid, and even a comic carving of a
woman beating her husband with a ladle.

ST MARY'S CHURCH *c1965* N3047

This view shows Gilbert Scott's west front from beyond the
Square. This is a church that mingles ancient and modern
perfectly. Indeed, my favourite window in the church is one
depicting the Creation that was only made in 1985: it is dedicated
to the memory of a local farmer, who can be seen amongst the
birds and animals walking his dog.

HIGH STREET *1898* 42179

This part of the town was devastated by the 1583 fire, so that everything here was built after that date. For instance, the timber building on the right was built the following year. It has an inscription that reads:

God grant our ryal Queen

In England longe to raign

For she hath put her helping

Hand to bild this town again.

▶ **THE SQUARE**
c1965 N3041

A comparison of this picture with the earlier one taken in 1898 (picture 42179, opposite) shows that nothing has really changed here other than the volume of traffic - even the blinds seem to have survived! The rebuilding of Nantwich after the fire was so effective that in 1620 the town was described as 'very fair and neat and every street adorned with some special mansions of gentlemen of good worth.'

◀ **HIGH STREET**
1898 42180

Here we have a closer look at the four-gabled house in picture 42179 (pages 16-17) – it originally comprised two houses. One of them was then occupied by a mercer (a dealer in fine cloth) called Thomas Church, and the other by his nephew, William. By the late 1800s there were three shops here; one of them, Grice the chemist's (in the centre), was to occupy these premises for many years to come.

HIGH STREET
c1965 N3065

Chatwins, the baker's and confectioner's (right), was founded in Nantwich by John Chatwin in 1913. Today the company has grown considerably - it now has 18 shops in Cheshire and Staffordshire, and employs over 300 people.

► **BARKER STREET**
1898 42182

This old building has now gone. The name 'Barker Street' recalls the tanning industry that used to be important in Nantwich; the bark from oak trees was used in the tanning process.

THE SHOPPING CENTRE
c1965 N3072

Although it looks very quiet in this view, this area of shops in the heart of Nantwich is one of the few with busy traffic constantly passing through. Woolworth's and Boots (both on the left) are still to be found here. Boots was previously on the corner of Hospital Street, as we can see in photograph N3053, opposite.

HOSPITAL STREET
c1965 N3053

The Lamb Hotel, in the centre of the picture, was built in 1861, and is currently being converted into flats. The first inn of that name in the street was established in 1552 by William Chatterton, once Groom in Ordinary to Queen Mary. It was later used as their headquarters by the Parliamentary forces during the siege of the town in the Civil War.

◀ **CHURCHES MANSION**
1898 42184

Standing just beyond Hospital Street, and therefore originally outside the town, this building also survived the fire. A carved inscription on the front of the building tells us that at the time of the fire it had just been built (some six years previously in 1577) for a wealthy merchant named Rychard Churche and his wife, Margerye, by Thomas Clease, the carpenter.

◄ **SWEET BRIAR HALL**
1898 42183

This building has now had all its plaster removed, so that the black and white timberwork below is revealed today. Built in the 15th century, it survived the fire of 1583, and is probably therefore the oldest timber building in the town. It was occupied in the mid-1700s by Joseph Priestley: he was a Unitarian minister, and also the discoverer of oxygen.

▲ **CHURCHES MANSION** *c1965* N3062

Used as a girl's school in the early 1900s, Churches Mansion was on the verge of being demolished when it was saved in 1930 by Edgar Myott, who began restoration work. By the time this photograph was taken, the building was being used as a restaurant. Today it houses an antiques business.

◄ **THE BRINE BATHS HOTEL** *1898* 42185

When 'Old Biot', as the large salt pit in Nantwich was known, was abandoned in 1856, it was later cleaned and reopened as a brine spring for medicinal treatments. The Brine Baths Hotel was then built to cater for those who visited the town for this purpose; here people could be treated for all manner of ills, from gout to rheumatism and even insomnia.

▶ **THE BRINE BATHS HOTEL**
1898 42186

The hotel's grounds covered 70 acres, so that with the decline in interest in medicinal treatments following the Second World War they became a prime site for development. Today new housing estates cover the area, with just the name 'Brine Road' to remind us of what was once here.

◀ **WELSH ROW**
1898 42181

Welsh Row is the name of the street leading westwards from Nantwich towards Wales. In medieval times it was called 'le Frog Row', which was apparently a reference to the open sewer that then ran down the centre of the street. Here we are looking eastwards, with the church tower in the distance.

▲ **WELSH ROW** *c1965* N3042

Nikolaus Pevsner describes Welsh Row as 'the best street in Nantwich', and the variety of buildings we can see in this photograph goes a long way to explaining why. There is a wonderful mixture of timber-framed, Georgian and Victorian buildings here, which line both sides of the road.

THE CHESHIRE CAT *c1965* N3036

Although immortalised by Lewis Carroll in *Alice in Wonderland*, the origins of the cat are said to go way back in time, and no-one knows where the story of the grinning cat, now always associated with Cheshire, originally came from. This building was built as three cottages in 1637; it was converted into almshouses before becoming a pub in 1945. It is no longer called The Cheshire Cat, which is sad.

◄ **WELSH ROW**
c1965 N3070

Walking along the street and noting the names of some of the cottages (Shoemakers and Tanners, for example), one is reminded of another important local industry – leather and the production of boots and shoes. By 1880, over 400,000 pairs of shoes and boots were being produced in Nantwich each year.

◀ **WELSH ROW**
c1965 N3066

The three-storey black and white building on the left of the picture is The Wilbraham Arms, named for an important local family who lived in nearby Dorfold Hall; the Wilbrahams were great benefactors to the town, establishing almshouses and schools here.

▲ **WELSH ROW,** *Old Cottages c1965* N3040

This building is now slightly shorter, and has been restored as a single cottage rather than the row of up to four dwellings pictured here. Its present name also reminds us of another old local industry: it is now called Malthouse Cottage.

◀ **WELSH ROW**
The Tollemache Almshouses c1965
N3039

Built in 1870 to replace the earlier Wilbraham almshouses, these delightful cottages are said to stand on a site originally used for a leper hospital founded here in the 13th century. This would make sense, as in those days such a hospital would need to have been some short distance from the community it served, and this site would have then been well outside the town.

BASIN END
The Shropshire Union Canal c1965
N3049

The Shropshire Union Canal, or 'Shroppie' as it is often known, is an amalgamation of many small canal companies extending over much of Cheshire; it was built to link the county primarily with the industrial centres of Birmingham and the Black Country and with the port of Liverpool. Today it serves the pleasure boat industry instead.

THE ENTRANCE GATES TO DORFOLD HALL *1898* 42193

Dorfold Hall was built for Ralph Wilbraham between the years 1616 and 1621, although the lodge house, shown here, dates from 1862. Despite being used by Parliamentarian soldiers during the Civil War as a site from which to bombard Nantwich, Dorfold Hall fortunately survives as one of the finest houses of its period in Cheshire.

DORFOLD HALL *1898* 42194

The Great Chamber of Dorfold Hall is particularly fine with its panelling and a stunning plaster ceiling. The ceiling is covered with fleurs-de-lis, thistles and roses, symbols of the royal houses of England and Scotland. Wilbraham was hoping that the King, James I, would visit, but he never did come.

▶ **DORFOLD HALL**
1898 42196

Today the park is still used each year for the Nantwich Show. The show is particularly famous for its cheese section, which is said to be the biggest in the world; it recalls a time when most farms locally would have produced their own cheese, which could not be 'equalled by any other made in Europe, for pleasantness of taste, and wholesomeness of digestion.'

◀ **ACTON**
St Mary's Church 1898
42197

Established in 1180 by the monks at nearby Combermere Abbey, St Mary's was sometimes used as a safe house when the Welsh were raiding the area. History was to repeat itself during the Civil War, when with fighting all around, the local vicar buried the church's silver somewhere near here. Unfortunately, he died before he had the chance to dig it up once more, and it has never been found!

▲ **ACTON,** *The Church c1960* A359002

In 1882 England played Australia in a cricket match; they lost so disastrously that they then ceremoniously burned the bails used during the match. Ever since then, Australia and England have played for 'the Ashes'. The captain in 1882 was Albert Hornby, and he is buried here. He was also the first man ever to captain England at both cricket and rugby.

◀ **ACTON**
The Star Inn c1960
A359001

The Star Inn has changed little over the years; it even still has its old mounting block attached to the front of the building. The cottage next door is part of the Dorfold Hall estate, which lies between Acton and Nantwich amongst the trees beyond.

CREWE

THE STATION *c1965* C316097

Many people may not know this town, but sooner or later everyone passes through 'one of the best known railway stations in the country'. The railway came to Crewe in 1837 with a line linking Warrington and Birmingham; the station here was then just a small halt station known as Woodnets Green.

BY COMPARISON with Nantwich, Crewe is a very modern town. Its name tells us that it was once known for a fish trap or weir somewhere in the vicinity; until a little over 150 years ago, it was never more than a small hamlet.

It was the introduction of the railways that made the town of Crewe. In fact, when the idea of a railway line (in this case linking Warrington with Birmingham) was first mooted, the original intention was that it should go via Nantwich. However, the people of Nantwich had only just got a new canal, and so they (and particularly those men who controlled the canal) saw no reason to build a new railway there as well; they did not want the railway to compete with what was a very effective means of transporting their goods.

And so the decision was made to put the new line through Crewe, where, fortunately for the railway builders, land was much cheaper anyway. When this decision was made in 1831, there were only 148 people living in Crewe. By the end of the century there were over 40,000 people living here, nearly a quarter of whom were linked in one way or another with the railway industry.

That first railway line (the Grand Junction) was opened in 1837. In 1840 this line was linked with a line to Chester; two years later another line was added that went to Manchester, and then later lines connected to Stoke on Trent and Shrewsbury. Thus Crewe very quickly became a major railway intersection.

But the town would never have grown as it did had it not been for the decision by the Grand Junction Railway Company in 1843 to found a locomotive production works here, too. The railway works were eventually to cover over 138 acres of land, and of these, 48 acres were under cover in the form of vast workshops. When in 1900 the 4,000th train left the production line here, such was the pride in this achievement that the workers were given a paid holiday, unheard of in those days.

The Grand Junction Railway Company was not only a railway company. It would probably be more accurate to say that it was the town. It was the company that built many houses and churches, and then laid on gas and water supplies. And it was the company that established Queen's Park in the year of Queen Victoria's golden jubilee, which was also, of course, the 50th anniversary of the opening of that first railway. Crewe's mayor who presided over that opening ceremony was known as the 'uncrowned king of Crewe'; his name was Frank Webb, and he was also the Chief Mechanical Engineer at the Crewe Railway Works.

At that time, faith in the future of the railway and the prosperity it would bring to the town must have been overwhelming. But as we know now, motor cars and aeroplanes were soon to be invented. Just as the railways had previously competed with the canals, so these new methods of transport would bring competition to the railways.

By the 1930s the number of men required locally in the railway industry was in steep decline. Fortunately, this skilled workforce was exactly what the new aero engine industry required, and so in 1938 Rolls Royce set up production here. Throughout the Second World War the company produced engines for Spitfires, Hurricanes, Lancasters and Mosquitoes.

After the war production was changed to cars, so that to this day the town is associated with the finest cars in the world. Strangely enough, despite this association with cars, it is said that Crewe has the highest number of cyclists for a town of its size in all of Britain.

Like other towns around the country where production has all tended to be concentrated in one business, recent years have seen a much-needed diversification in local industry. Fortunately, from the point of view of the town's economic survival, Crewe has from its earliest days benefited from good communications. Today, with the addition of nearby motorways and airports, Crewe is still ideally positioned for the development of numerous industries; its survival as a vibrant town is therefore assured.

THE STATION
c1965 C316104

Following the development of more lines through here, the present station was built in 1845-46 - the canopy was added in 1848. Together with the railway works and sidings, the original track through the town was eventually to develop to the point that at its peak, there was over 70 miles of railway track in Crewe!

CHRIST CHURCH *c1950* C316015

On seeing the ruined shell of this church today, the visitor may
well get the immediate impression that it must have suffered
from bombing during the war; but in fact the nave was
demolished in 1977 because of dry rot in the roof, and today only
the chancel end is still used. The church was originally built by
the Grand Junction Railway Company in 1845. The tower, with its
beautiful terracotta detail, was designed by the company
engineer J W Stansby; it was added in 1877.

MARKET STREET *c1955* C316032

This shot was taken at the southern end of Market Street, which leads to that area of town that was traditionally the main shopping centre. Shoppers still congregate at the other end of the street to this day (in a shopping precinct opened by the Queen in 1955, and therefore called Queensway), while this part has become rather run-down by comparison.

THE SQUARE
c1955 C316023

Before reaching the main market or shopping area, however, we pass the wide, open square. It was the officials of the Grand Junction railway that insisted that this space should be left unoccupied, and it was then used as a market square. Today this scene is little changed, except that traffic now travels along only two sides of the square - along Delamere Street in the foreground, and Market Street at the far end.

41

THE SQUARE
c1955 C316037

Visitors to the town would normally expect the Square in Crewe to be the centre of the town, and correspondingly busy; but with the shift of the heart of the shopping area further north, I doubt whether this area would see many shoppers at all were it not for the presence of Marks & Spencer (right). Notice the blinds over the windows, which have since all been bricked up.

MARKET SQUARE *c1960* C316063

This view shows the Square a few years after No C316037 (above) was taken. The road system around the Square is beginning to be changed, with one side of the street now closed to regular traffic. Another major change in the years since has been the replacement of all the buildings along the left-hand side of the street.

THE TOWN CENTRE *c1955* C316035

Historians of the future will generally not thank the architects of 1950s and 1960s Britain for their contributions to our towns and cities, and this stark, utilitarian building explains exactly why! The clock tower is known to the locals as 'Big Bill'.

THE TOWN CENTRE *c1955* C316036
The name Odeon is said by some to stand for 'Oscar Deutsch
Entertains Our Nation'. However, this is no longer the case here,
as the cinema was demolished in 1983. Enlargement of the bill-
board over the entrance shows us that the film then showing was
Friendly Persuasion, starring Gary Cooper.

THE WAR MEMORIAL *c1960* C316066a

The Square is dominated by Crewe's war memorial, which is a very grand affair; so it should be – it commemorates so many people from the town. An idea of the number of people remembered can be gained when we consider that each metal plaque around the statue (just behind the seats where people are sitting) lists the people who died, and there are several of these plaques.

THE BUS STATION
c1960 C316055

Situated just behind the clock tower, the bus station was opened in 1960 on a site that had previously been occupied by houses for railway workers. Now it is extremely run-down, with all the walls covered in graffiti. Notice the steeple of St Paul's Church in the distance (centre) – it was taken down soon after the bus station opened.

THE BUS STATION
c1960 C316043

The thing that strikes me most when I look at this photograph is how much more smartly everyone dressed in those days than we do today, even if they were just coming into town to do some shopping. Society generally may be much more affluent these days than 50 years ago, but in this respect at least, a visitor from outer space would be hard put to recognise the fact.

MARKET STREET *c1960* C316067

Returning to the Square, we are once again looking at Market Street. The main change that immediately strikes the visitor today is that the lovely old Victorian Barclays Bank building (right) has gone, to be replaced by yet another typical 1960s monstrosity. What were the town planners doing? Surely they could at least have kept the old façade. Many other buildings further up the street have also been replaced.

MARKET STREET *c1965* C316099

One of the new buildings at the end of Market Street is this one – Boots, the chemists. This company was founded in Nottingham in the 1870s by Jesse Boot. From a small shop selling herbal remedies in the poorest area of Nottingham, within 20 years he had established a business with 60 shops in nearly 30 towns.

MARKET HALL C316011a

The market hall was built by John Hill in 1854. It should come as no surprise in Crewe that he was a railway contractor for the London and North Western Railway (LNWR). Intended as a cheese market, it had a capacity for 2,000 tons of cheese. Originally it had direct access at the rear of the building to the main railway line.

MARKET HALL
Earle Street c1955
This is a close up of photograph C316011a (page 50) – notice the advertisement on the left behind the gentleman. It reads: 'Ruptured yet never a care – thanks to my Brooks Rupture Appliance'. It does make me wonder why we do not see posters like this any more. Has the medical treatment of ruptures changed?

THE CHETWODE ARMS AND ST PAUL'S CHURCH *c1950* C316013

Designed by J W Stansby (who also designed the tower of Christ Church), St Paul's was built in 1868-69 at the expense of the Grand Junction Railway Company. The spire was added in 1888. Today it is only the tall tower (now without its spire) that enables the visitor to work out where this picture was taken. The church building is now used by the charity Christian Concern, and the building is actually used as a centre for second-hand furniture. It is known as St Paul's Centre.

▼ THE CHETWODE ARMS *c1960* C316024

The Chetwode Arms once stood opposite St Paul's Church, but it was demolished when West Street was widened for the building of a dual carriageway here. The building was reputed to date from 1620, and the local people held demonstrations to try and stop the demolition, but such is the road to progress …

► QUEEN'S PARK

c1960 C316061

Queen's Park was presented to the town by the London North Western Railway Company (LNWR) in 1887, and marked not only the Queen's Jubilee (hence the park's name), but also the 50th anniversary of the opening of the Grand Junction Railway in Crewe, which could be said to be the reason for the town's very existence.

◄ QUEEN'S PARK
The Main Entrance c1950
C316002

The clock tower stands just inside the main entrance to Queen's Park. It was built using subscriptions from workers in all departments of the LNWR Company 'as a token of their appreciation of the generosity of their Board of Directors (who) presented the park to the town'. It is decorated with a carved head on each side depicting three board members and Queen Victoria. It also served as a drinking fountain, but the water has now been cut off.

► QUEEN'S PARK
The Gardens and Lake c1960 C316083

Notice how immaculate the grounds are, and the numerous small flower beds all planted out with annuals. Maintaining gardens such as this is extremely labour intensive, and it is prohibitively expensive in today's world; now nearly all the flower beds have gone, to be replaced by open lawns and shrubs.

QUEEN'S PARK *c1960* C316050

This view looks up towards the old Pavilion, which was built in
1887. Unfortunately it was destroyed by fire in 1972, so that today
a new pavilion stands on this site. The new pavilion continues the
tradition here of commemorating a Queen's jubilee: it is called
the Jubilee Pavilion, and it was built in 1977 to celebrate our
present Queen Elizabeth's 25th year on the throne.

QUEEN'S PARK
*The Lake and the
Pavilion c1960* C316081

There are some interesting memorials in the park. A particularly fine one is situated just behind the Pavilion building: it was erected to commemorate those soldiers from the town who fought in the Boer War in South Africa. It is particularly interesting in that it lists all the soldiers who served there, not just those who died. A very recent memorial in the park is dedicated to Diana, Princess of Wales – as a work of art I feel it leaves much to be desired.

QUEEN'S PARK, *The Lake and the Bridge c1950* C316005

Another interesting memorial in the park is the dedication on the island in the middle of the lake. It is actually the island garden that is dedicated, and it remembers all soldiers (not just those from Crewe) who served in the South East Asia Command and who died in the Burma Campaign in the Second World War – the island is therefore known as the Burma Star Island.

QUEEN'S PARK
The Lake 1951 C316006

I think this is a particularly charming photograph of the boating lake in the park. One of the men pictured on the right is brushing the hull of an upturned boat which, presumably, will soon be available for hire once again. The second man is obviously the foreman: he is standing watching, with his hands on his hips!

◄ QUEEN'S PARK
c1965 C316087

The bowling green, which we see here in the foreground, still survives. But foreign sports are taking over: just beyond the hedge today a strip of land has been prepared with sand so that people can play boules. When considering sporting interests in the town, it is interesting to note that Crewe's football club, Crewe Alexandra, is the oldest club in the Football League, having been founded in 1876.

◄ QUEEN'S PARK
*The Lake and
the Bridge c1950*
C316004

The lake was not just used for boating. In the early 1900s part of it was set aside for swimmers, and it was used for this purpose until proper swimming baths were built in Crewe and opened in 1937.

▲ **WISTASTON,** *The Rectory c1960* W502062

Situated just beyond Queen's Park, Wistaston is now a suburb of the town of Crewe. John Gerard, born in Nantwich in 1545, was educated in this village. Later to become a herbalist and surgeon in London, he is famous for a book of herbal remedies in which he was the first to refer to plants by their English rather than Latin names.

**◄ THE ROLLS ROYCE
WORKS**
c1955 C316029

Although it was undoubtedly the railways that first brought heavy industry to the region (indeed, they were for a long time the major employers in the town), it was not long before other industries associated with engines and heavy machinery followed. The most famous of these was Rolls Royce, shown here, whose Aero Engine factory was established in 1938.

▶ **THE ROLLS ROYCE WORKS**
c1965 C316092

Ten years have passed since No C316029, (page 59) was taken, and nothing has changed except that the window frames have been painted white. After the Second World War, it was for the production of cars that this factory became especially famous; for a time road signs in the vicinity all advertised 'Crewe and Nantwich – Home of the Best Car in the World.'

◀ **THE ROLLS ROYCE WORKS**
c1965 C316093

Times change, however, and motor production companies seem to be regularly changing hands today. The name on the wall here now reads 'Bentley Motors', and the crest over the main entrance has also been changed. Also, there is now a smart new awning over the entrance. Mind you, although they built Rolls-Royces, it is evident that the employees did not appear to drive them!

▲ THE TEACHERS' TRAINING COLLEGE *c1965* C316110

The first teacher training college was established in Crewe in 1908, and moved here in 1912. At first a mixed college for primary and secondary school teachers, it then became a women's college for teachers for primary and nursery schools only, with an associated college for male teachers at nearby Alsager.

◄ THE TEACHERS' TRAINING COLLEGE *c1965* C316095

Today the college is mixed once more. It is now part of the Manchester Metropolitan University, and it is still linked with the campus at Alsager, as well as with five other campus sites in the Manchester area. The sites at Crewe and Alsager are home to around 3,500 students, with almost a third of them attending postgraduate courses; some still train here to become teachers.

AROUND NANTWICH AND CREWE

WRENBURY, *The Green c1955* W414006

Overlooking the village green is St Margaret's Church. One notable curiosity inside is the old dog whipper's pew. Paid a few shillings each year (and given a coat and hat), his job was to keep all the dogs under control and also to ensure that the congregation stayed awake. Let us hope that he used a tickling stick for this purpose (as was the norm) rather than his whip.

IN THEIR DIFFERENT WAYS, the two towns of Nantwich and Crewe have both developed because of their association with very specialised industries: salt and the production of locomotives. Yet a short walk from either town brings the visitor into a rural setting that seems a million miles from any industry at all.

This is the area of the county that is known as the Cheshire Plain, and it is famous for a totally different commodity – cheese. For centuries, Cheshire cheese was produced on nearly every farm in the region, and these matured cheeses would then have been brought in to market, particularly to Nantwich, where an annual cheese fair was established in 1820. Production of this farm-produced cheese peaked in 1907, when 600,000 cwt was produced locally. However, the next year was to see the introduction of factory-produced cheese.

Today there is only one farm left where the production of Cheshire cheese is totally bound to one farm, all the way from the breeding of the cows for the right milk to the maturing of the final cheese – and it is not even in Cheshire, but just over the border in northern Shropshire. But technically at least it is still in the Cheshire Plain region!

But the walker wandering along the many footpaths through the fields here is still going to be aware of the importance of cattle in the agricultural community, although probably remaining unaware of the fact that the milk they provide is all sent to factories for processing. Also, more and more of the farmhouses he or she will pass are now homes for people whose livelihood is provided elsewhere, usually in the towns, to which local people commute.

As well as most locals working in the towns, children now attend secondary schools in the towns, and people do more and more of their shopping in the towns, so that village shops are forced to close down. It is a sad fact that this often leads to a decline in the spirit of villages and smaller towns; but this does not seem to be the case in this part of the world, where many small towns and villages are still very vibrant communities.

The photographs of the towns and villages that follow are only a sample of those to be found in this region, but all of them share this strong community spirit.

HASLINGTON, *High Street c1955* H324005

WRENBURY
The Doctor's House
c1955 W414005

So-called because it was occupied by a doctor in the early 1900s, this house is now known as Stanley House. Just under the large gable there is a plaque which gives the date 1859, and a close inspection of the building reveals that despite first appearances, this is not a timber building at all, but brick that has been painted black and white.

WRENBURY
The School c1955
W414009

Nikolaus Pevsner describes this schoolhouse as 'brick, gothic and very idiosyncratic'. Typical of 19th-century schoolhouses up and down the country, it has a particularly moving war memorial to those local boys killed in the First World War, which reads: 'The blood of heroes is the seed of freedom.'

WRENBURY
The Canal c1955
W414011

The lift bridge here is one of only two in the whole country that are used to carry regular traffic over a canal (in this case the Shropshire Union Canal); it is regulated by a set of traffic lights. The large barn on the right was converted into a pub called The Dusty Miller in 1970, while the building on the left is an office and shop for holiday boating traffic.

MARBURY
The Church and the Mere 1898 42478

This is another extremely pretty little village in the heart of what was once Cheshire's cheese-producing countryside. Milk is still produced here, but the cheese is now made in local factories rather than on the farms. With farming in decline in the years after the Second World War, much land locally was sold in 1945, and is now owned by the Duchy of Lancaster.

MARBURY, *The Church 1898* 42480

If you look closely at St Michael's Church, you might think you see a slight lean of the tower - and you could be right. Built on sandstone with a mere just below it, the church has slipped slightly over the years; today the 63ft tower apparently tilts more than two feet out of the vertical. There is a local legend that says that if the ancient yew tree in the churchyard falls, so will the church ...

BEESTON, *The Castle c1960* B57008

The site now occupied by this ruined castle was first fortified over 2,000 years ago by the ancient Britons. Built as one of a series defending the English border from Welsh attack, the castle had already fallen into disrepair by the 1600s, when it was refortified during the Civil War. After changing hands a couple of times during that war, it was finally slighted in 1645.

BUNBURY, *Tudor Cottage c1960* B562009

Bunbury has been described as 'a village that the commuter has found but not spoilt', and it has a delightful mixture of buildings of all periods. The village itself is rather a tale of two halves: this area around the former village green has the shops, and the other half, a short distance away, is focused on the church.

BUNBURY
The Village c1960
B562016

And this is, or rather was, the village green. The house in the centre was built in 1831. It incorporates what was once the village lock-up, with the old cells now forming part of the entrance hall – what a way to welcome your guests!

BUNBURY, *The Nag's Head Hotel c1960* B562023

Bunbury is still a thriving community with its village shops and pubs, but it is still vastly different from the 1920s, when there were 14 shops and even two banks still here.

BUNBURY
The Dysart Arms
c1960 B562007

During the Second World War the nearby town of Crewe was a prime target for air attacks, and nearby villages did not escape. In 1940 bombs fell in this part of the village, and the church was nearly destroyed. Barrage balloons were used to try and protect Crewe, but these were not always successful – on one occasion a direct hit on the Rolls Royce works killed 16 workers.

CHURCH MINSHULL, *St Bartholomew's Church c1955* C478003

The people of this village were so poor that when they needed to rebuild the church, Queen Anne herself provided money for it. The date, 1702, can be seen in different coloured bricks on the tower. They might have been poor, but they must have been healthy – church registers record a John Damme who died in 1649 aged 'seven score and fourteene' and a James Archer who died in 1771 aged 105.

CHURCH MINSHULL, *Church Farm c1955* C478011

This was once the home of Elizabeth Minshull, the third wife of the poet John Milton. Local wags will tell you that he married her for her money, and then promptly left her here while he returned to London. In fact she married him in London in 1663, and they lived in Buckinghamshire until his death in 1674. During this period, already blind, Milton wrote his most famous works: *Paradise Lost, Paradise Regained* and *Samson Agonistes*. At the time of her own death in 1727, Elizabeth was living in Nantwich.

CHURCH MINSHULL, *The Post Office c1955* C478002

This view shows the same telephone exchange cottage that we saw in C478012, above, but from the other direction. The post office (and village shop) is the building on the far right of the photograph; it was run by 'the redoubtable Miss Brereton' before the First World War. It is now a private house.

CHURCH MINSHULL
The Main Street c1955
C478012

The building on the right has gone, to be replaced by four small bungalows for the elderly, built rather further back from the road. Notice the telephone kiosk on the other side of the road. The cottage just beyond was once the home of Miss Egerton who ran the local telephone exchange from here, but it too has now been replaced by a rather more standardised building.

CHURCH MINSHULL, *The Old Mill c1955* C478006

Now used as a forge, the old mill was originally used for the grinding of corn. The old water wheel in the mill was also used to provide electricity for the whole village, which only joined the National Grid in around 1960. Miss Billenge, who then ran the mill, always kept the wheels turning to provide the power, although at times lights would flicker throughout the village if too much power was being used at any one time.

HASLINGTON
High Street c1955
H324005

The garage in the centre of the photograph has been demolished to make way for a new post office and convenience store, but the building in the foreground, the Cosey Social Club, still remains. Another centre for socialising is the pub – the building with the white gable end beyond the garage. As a collector of pub signs, I find its sign, depicting a fox cub in the snow, particularly appealing.

▶ **HASLINGTON**
High Street c1955
H324004

The delightful timber-framed house in the centre of the picture is said to date from 1510. Notice the telephone box just beyond – many of the earliest public telephones were set up inside private houses, and there used to be one inside this particular cottage. The building on the far right of the picture has now gone – this is now the entrance into a new housing estate behind.

◀ **HASLINGTON**
The Village c1955
H324002

The Hawk Inn is pictured here (centre). It has now had the plaster removed to reveal timber work, and is also dated to 1510. Inscribed on timbers around it are the words 'a jug of ale (and) a whispered word can be found within these old walls', and it advertises 'good ale and dry stables'. Dick Turpin is reputed to have once stabled his horse here.

▲ **HASLINGTON,** *Main Road c1960* H324016

This former dairy factory, Whey Products, which was situated just on the northern edge of the village, has now gone; the land has also been used for a new housing estate.

◀ **SANDBACH**
Old Houses,
Front Street c1955
S489001

This view shows a row of the most delightful cottages just below the church. At the end of the row there is a pipe with water still issuing from it: this is the source from which the townspeople used to get all their water. Notice that it is just below the graveyard – not (I would think) the best place to get your drinking water!

SANDBACH
St Mary's Church
c1960 S489031

For those people who enjoy exploring churchyards and reading old tombstones, this church is an absolute joy. The entire churchyard, and even the paths leading to the door, are all covered with tombstones, some of which date back to the 1600s. Despite centuries of wear, they are still remarkably legible; furthermore, many have been carved to an extremely high standard with the most beautiful lettering.

SANDBACH, *Ancient Saxon Crosses c1955* S489016

Despite the fact that most of our towns and villages were founded in Saxon times, few have any reminders of their Saxon history left other than perhaps their names. Here, however, there are the shafts of two stunningly beautiful Saxon crosses. The taller one is covered with scenes from the life of Christ, whilst the smaller one is thought to depict scenes from the life of King Penda of Mercia (whose territory this once was). He was converted to Christianity some time around AD653.

SANDBACH
The War Memorial
c1955 S489005

The old Saxon crosses stand in the Market Square. Here today there is another stone memorial, this time dedicated to those who fell in the First and Second World Wars. I cannot help but wonder if it, too, will survive for over 1,300 years; I like to think so.

SANDBACH, *The Black Bear Inn c1955* S489007

Overlooking the Market Square is the Black Bear Inn. The building dates from 1634. Today the ground floor has been painted white, so that the timberwork can only be seen on the floor above. The cobbles in the foreground can just be distinguished in the photograph – it is amazing that these still survive to add to the charm of the entire square.

SANDBACH
*The Lower Chequer
Inn c1965* S489047

We get our word
'exchequer' from the fact
that money used to be
counted out on cloths or
tables marked out in a
chequered pattern.
Traditionally, pubs that
bear this name were
places where people
could get loans or
exchange money, so it is
no surprise to find that
this pub is just beside the
Market Square. The
building dates from 1570.

ALSAGER, *Crewe Road c1965* A214002

Listed in the *Domesday Book* as 'Eleacier', the town's name tells us that this was once 'Aelle's field or ploughed land'. But it
may be that the final element of the name comes from the Norse word 'akr', indicating Viking settlement here – the Vikings
certainly inhabited the county around Chester, but we will never know for sure if they settled this far inland. 'Akr' is also the
source of our word 'acre' today.

ALSAGER, *Crewe Road c1965* A214021

For centuries the town was little more than a small agricultural hamlet. Then the Alsager family started to build houses and a church here in the 18th and 19th centuries. This view shows the main road through the town, which has changed little in recent years.

ALSAGER
Sandbach Road
c1960 A214011

The cyclists pictured on the road have just crossed over the railway line; this crossing is now controlled by traffic lights. The railway came to Alsager in 1848 with a line linking Crewe and Derby, and within two years there were five trains daily on this line that called at Alsager.

ALSAGER, *Hassall Road c1955* A214005

This road is a very busy one today, as it leads to the Alsager campus of Manchester Metropolitan University. The building on the right in the photograph is the Methodist church. It was built in 1834 on what would then have been the very outskirts of the town.

INDEX

Frith Book Co Titles

www.francisfrith.co.uk

The Frith Book Company publishes over 100 new titles each year. A selection of those currently available is listed below. For latest catalogue please contact Frith Book Co.

Town Books 96 pages, approximately 100 photos. **County and Themed Books** 128 pages, approximately 150 photos (unless specified). All titles hardback with laminated case and jacket, except those indicated pb (paperback)

Title	ISBN	Price	Title	ISBN	Price
Amersham, Chesham & Rickmansworth (pb)	1-85937-340-2	£9.99	Devon (pb)	1-85937-297-x	£9.99
Andover (pb)	1-85937-292-9	£9.99	Devon Churches (pb)	1-85937-250-3	£9.99
Aylesbury (pb)	1-85937-227-9	£9.99	Dorchester (pb)	1-85937-307-0	£9.99
Barnstaple (pb)	1-85937-300-3	£9.99	Dorset (pb)	1-85937-269-4	£9.99
Basildon Living Memories (pb)	1-85937-515-4	£9.99	Dorset Coast (pb)	1-85937-299-6	£9.99
Bath (pb)	1-85937-419-0	£9.99	Dorset Living Memories (pb)	1-85937-584-7	£9.99
Bedford (pb)	1-85937-205-8	£9.99	Down the Severn (pb)	1-85937-560-x	£9.99
Bedfordshire Living Memories	1-85937-513-8	£14.99	Down The Thames (pb)	1-85937-278-3	£9.99
Belfast (pb)	1-85937-303-8	£9.99	Down the Trent	1-85937-311-9	£14.99
Berkshire (pb)	1-85937-191-4	£9.99	East Anglia (pb)	1-85937-265-1	£9.99
Berkshire Churches	1-85937-170-1	£17.99	East Grinstead (pb)	1-85937-138-8	£9.99
Berkshire Living Memories	1-85937-332-1	£14.99	East London	1-85937-080-2	£14.99
Black Country	1-85937-497-2	£12.99	East Sussex (pb)	1-85937-606-1	£9.99
Blackpool (pb)	1-85937-393-3	£9.99	Eastbourne (pb)	1-85937-399-2	£9.99
Bognor Regis (pb)	1-85937-431-x	£9.99	Edinburgh (pb)	1-85937-193-0	£8.99
Bournemouth (pb)	1-85937-545-6	£9.99	England In The 1880s	1-85937-331-3	£17.99
Bradford (pb)	1-85937-204-x	£9.99	Essex - Second Selection	1-85937-456-5	£14.99
Bridgend (pb)	1-85937-386-0	£7.99	Essex (pb)	1-85937-270-8	£9.99
Bridgwater (pb)	1-85937-305-4	£9.99	Essex Coast	1-85937-342-9	£14.99
Bridport (pb)	1-85937-327-5	£9.99	Essex Living Memories	1-85937-490-5	£14.99
Brighton (pb)	1-85937-192-2	£8.99	Exeter	1-85937-539-1	£9.99
Bristol (pb)	1-85937-264-3	£9.99	Exmoor	1-85937-608-8	£9.99
British Life A Century Ago (pb)	1-85937-213-9	£9.99	Falmouth (pb)	1-85937-594-4	£9.99
Buckinghamshire (pb)	1-85937-200-7	£9.99	Folkestone (pb)	1-85937-124-8	£9.99
Camberley (pb)	1-85937-222-8	£9.99	Frome (pb)	1-85937-317-8	£9.99
Cambridge (pb)	1-85937-422-0	£9.99	Glamorgan	1-85937-488-3	£14.99
Cambridgeshire (pb)	1-85937-420-4	£9.99	Glasgow (pb)	1-85937-190-6	£9.99
Cambridgeshire Villages	1-85937-523-5	£14.99	Glastonbury (pb)	1-85937-338-0	£7.99
Canals And Waterways (pb)	1-85937-291-0	£9.99	Gloucester (pb)	1-85937-232-5	£9.99
Canterbury Cathedral (pb)	1-85937-179-5	£9.99	Gloucestershire (pb)	1-85937-561-8	£9.99
Cardiff (pb)	1-85937-093-4	£9.99	Great Yarmouth (pb)	1-85937-426-3	£9.99
Carmarthenshire (pb)	1-85937-604-5	£9.99	Greater Manchester (pb)	1-85937-266-x	£9.99
Chelmsford (pb)	1-85937-310-0	£9.99	Guildford (pb)	1-85937-410-7	£9.99
Cheltenham (pb)	1-85937-095-0	£9.99	Hampshire (pb)	1-85937-279-1	£9.99
Cheshire (pb)	1-85937-271-6	£9.99	Harrogate (pb)	1-85937-423-9	£9.99
Chester (pb)	1-85937-382 8	£9.99	Hastings and Bexhill (pb)	1-85937-131-0	£9.99
Chesterfield (pb)	1-85937-378-x	£9.99	Heart of Lancashire (pb)	1-85937-197-3	£9.99
Chichester (pb)	1-85937-228-7	£9.99	Helston (pb)	1-85937-214-7	£9.99
Churches of East Cornwall (pb)	1-85937-249-x	£9.99	Hereford (pb)	1-85937-175-2	£9.99
Churches of Hampshire (pb)	1-85937-207-4	£9.99	Herefordshire (pb)	1-85937-567-7	£9.99
Cinque Ports & Two Ancient Towns	1-85937-492-1	£14.99	Herefordshire Living Memories	1-85937-514-6	£14.99
Colchester (pb)	1-85937-188-4	£8.99	Hertfordshire (pb)	1-85937-247-3	£9.99
Cornwall (pb)	1-85937-229-5	£9.99	Horsham (pb)	1-85937-432-8	£9.99
Cornwall Living Memories	1-85937-248-1	£14.99	Humberside (pb)	1-85937-605-3	£9.99
Cotswolds (pb)	1-85937-230-9	£9.99	Hythe, Romney Marsh, Ashford (pb)	1-85937-256-2	£9.99
Cotswolds Living Memories	1-85937-255-4	£14.99	Ipswich (pb)	1-85937-424-7	£9.99
County Durham (pb)	1-85937-398-4	£9.99	Isle of Man (pb)	1-85937-268-6	£9.99
Croydon Living Memories (pb)	1-85937-162-0	£9.99	Isle of Wight (pb)	1-85937-429-8	£9.99
Cumbria (pb)	1-85937-621-5	£9.99	Isle of Wight Living Memories	1-85937-304-6	£14.99
Derby (pb)	1-85937-367-4	£9.99	Kent (pb)	1-85937-189-2	£9.99
Derbyshire (pb)	1-85937-196-5	£9.99	Kent Living Memories(pb)	1-85937-401-8	£9.99
Derbyshire Living Memories	1-85937-330-5	£14.99	Kings Lynn (pb)	1-85937-334-8	£9.99

Available from your local bookshop or from the publisher

Frith Book Co Titles (continued)

Title	ISBN	Price	Title	ISBN	Price
Lake District (pb)	1-85937-275-9	£9.99	Sherborne (pb)	1-85937-301-1	£9.99
Lancashire Living Memories	1-85937-335-6	£14.99	Shrewsbury (pb)	1-85937-325-9	£9.99
Lancaster, Morecambe, Heysham (pb)	1-85937-233-3	£9.99	Shropshire (pb)	1-85937-326-7	£9.99
Leeds (pb)	1-85937-202-3	£9.99	Shropshire Living Memories	1-85937-643-6	£14.99
Leicester (pb)	1-85937-381-x	£9.99	Somerset	1-85937-153-1	£14.99
Leicestershire & Rutland Living Memories	1-85937-500-6	£12.99	South Devon Coast	1-85937-107-8	£14.99
Leicestershire (pb)	1-85937-185-x	£9.99	South Devon Living Memories (pb)	1-85937-609-6	£9.99
Lighthouses	1-85937-257-0	£9.99	South East London (pb)	1-85937-263-5	£9.99
Lincoln (pb)	1-85937-380-1	£9.99	South Somerset	1-85937-318-6	£14.99
Lincolnshire (pb)	1-85937-433-6	£9.99	South Wales	1-85937-519-7	£14.99
Liverpool and Merseyside (pb)	1-85937-234-1	£9.99	Southampton (pb)	1-85937-427-1	£9.99
London (pb)	1-85937-183-3	£9.99	Southend (pb)	1-85937-313-5	£9.99
London Living Memories	1-85937-454-9	£14.99	Southport (pb)	1-85937-425-5	£9.99
Ludlow (pb)	1-85937-176-0	£9.99	St Albans (pb)	1-85937-341-0	£9.99
Luton (pb)	1-85937-235-x	£9.99	St Ives (pb)	1-85937-415-8	£9.99
Maidenhead (pb)	1-85937-339-9	£9.99	Stafford Living Memories (pb)	1-85937-503-0	£9.99
Maidstone (pb)	1-85937-391-7	£9.99	Staffordshire (pb)	1-85937-308-9	£9.99
Manchester (pb)	1-85937-198-1	£9.99	Stourbridge (pb)	1-85937-530-8	£9.99
Marlborough (pb)	1-85937-336-4	£9.99	Stratford upon Avon (pb)	1-85937-388-7	£9.99
Middlesex	1-85937-158-2	£14.99	Suffolk (pb)	1-85937-221-x	£9.99
Monmouthshire	1-85937-532-4	£14.99	Suffolk Coast (pb)	1-85937-610-x	£9.99
New Forest (pb)	1-85937-390-9	£9.99	Surrey (pb)	1-85937-240-6	£9.99
Newark (pb)	1-85937-366-6	£9.99	Surrey Living Memories	1-85937-328-3	£14.99
Newport, Wales (pb)	1-85937-258-9	£9.99	Sussex (pb)	1-85937-184-1	£9.99
Newquay (pb)	1-85937-421-2	£9.99	Sutton (pb)	1-85937-337-2	£9.99
Norfolk (pb)	1-85937-195-7	£9.99	Swansea (pb)	1-85937-167-1	£9.99
Norfolk Broads	1-85937-486-7	£14.99	Taunton (pb)	1-85937-314-3	£9.99
Norfolk Living Memories (pb)	1-85937-402-6	£9.99	Tees Valley & Cleveland (pb)	1-85937-623-1	£9.99
North Buckinghamshire	1-85937-626-6	£14.99	Teignmouth (pb)	1-85937-370-4	£7.99
North Devon Living Memories	1-85937-261-9	£14.99	Thanet (pb)	1-85937-116-7	£9.99
North Hertfordshire	1-85937-547-2	£14.99	Tiverton (pb)	1-85937-178-7	£9.99
North London (pb)	1-85937-403-4	£9.99	Torbay (pb)	1-85937-597-9	£9.99
North Somerset	1-85937-302-x	£14.99	Truro (pb)	1-85937-598-7	£9.99
North Wales (pb)	1-85937-298-8	£9.99	Victorian & Edwardian Dorset	1-85937-254-6	£14.99
North Yorkshire (pb)	1-85937-236-8	£9.99	Victorian & Edwardian Kent (pb)	1-85937-624-X	£9.99
Northamptonshire Living Memories	1-85937-529-4	£14.99	Victorian & Edwardian Maritime Album (pb)	1-85937-622-3	£9.99
Northamptonshire	1-85937-150-7	£14.99	Victorian and Edwardian Sussex (pb)	1-85937-625-8	£9.99
Northumberland Tyne & Wear (pb)	1-85937-281-3	£9.99	Villages of Devon (pb)	1-85937-293-7	£9.99
Northumberland	1-85937-522-7	£14.99	Villages of Kent (pb)	1-85937-294-5	£9.99
Norwich (pb)	1-85937-194-9	£8.99	Villages of Sussex (pb)	1-85937-295-3	£9.99
Nottingham (pb)	1-85937-324-0	£9.99	Warrington (pb)	1-85937-507-3	£9.99
Nottinghamshire (pb)	1-85937-187-6	£9.99	Warwick (pb)	1-85937-518-9	£9.99
Oxford (pb)	1-85937-411-5	£9.99	Warwickshire (pb)	1-85937-203-1	£9.99
Oxfordshire (pb)	1-85937-430-1	£9.99	Welsh Castles (pb)	1-85937-322-4	£9.99
Oxfordshire Living Memories	1-85937-525-1	£14.99	West Midlands (pb)	1-85937-289-9	£9.99
Paignton (pb)	1-85937-374-7	£7.99	West Sussex (pb)	1-85937-607-x	£9.99
Peak District (pb)	1-85937-280-5	£9.99	West Yorkshire (pb)	1-85937-201-5	£9.99
Pembrokeshire	1-85937-262-7	£14.99	Weston Super Mare (pb)	1-85937-306-2	£9.99
Penzance (pb)	1-85937-595-2	£9.99	Weymouth (pb)	1-85937-209-0	£9.99
Peterborough (pb)	1-85937-219-8	£9.99	Wiltshire (pb)	1-85937-277-5	£9.99
Picturesque Harbours	1-85937-208-2	£14.99	Wiltshire Churches (pb)	1-85937-171-x	£9.99
Piers	1-85937-237-6	£17.99	Wiltshire Living Memories (pb)	1-85937-396-8	£9.99
Plymouth (pb)	1-85937-389-5	£9.99	Winchester (pb)	1-85937-428-x	£9.99
Poole & Sandbanks (pb)	1-85937-251-1	£9.99	Windsor (pb)	1-85937-333-x	£9.99
Preston (pb)	1-85937-212-0	£9.99	Wokingham & Bracknell (pb)	1-85937-329-1	£9.99
Reading (pb)	1-85937-238-4	£9.99	Woodbridge (pb)	1-85937-498-0	£9.99
Redhill to Reigate (pb)	1-85937-596-0	£9.99	Worcester (pb)	1-85937-165-5	£9.99
Ringwood (pb)	1-85937-384-4	£7.99	Worcestershire Living Memories	1-85937-489-1	£14.99
Romford (pb)	1-85937-319-4	£9.99	Worcestershire	1-85937-152-3	£14.99
Royal Tunbridge Wells (pb)	1-85937-504-9	£9.99	York (pb)	1-85937-199-x	£9.99
Salisbury (pb)	1-85937-239-2	£9.99	Yorkshire (pb)	1-85937-186-8	£9.99
Scarborough (pb)	1-85937-379-8	£9.99	Yorkshire Coastal Memories	1-85937-506-5	£14.99
Sevenoaks and Tonbridge (pb)	1-85937-392-5	£9.99	Yorkshire Dales	1-85937-502-2	£14.99
Sheffield & South Yorks (pb)	1-85937-267-8	£9.99	Yorkshire Living Memories (pb)	1-85937-397-6	£9.99

See Frith books on the internet at www.francisfrith.co.uk

FRITH PRODUCTS & SERVICES

Francis Frith would doubtless be pleased to know that the pioneering publishing venture he started in 1860 still continues today. Over a hundred and forty years later, The Francis Frith Collection continues in the same innovative tradition and is now one of the foremost publishers of vintage photographs in the world. Some of the current activities include:

Interior Decoration

Today Frith's photographs can be seen framed and as giant wall murals in thousands of pubs, restaurants, hotels, banks, retail stores and other public buildings throughout the country. In every case they enhance the unique local atmosphere of the places they depict and provide reminders of gentler days in an increasingly busy and frenetic world.

Product Promotions

Frith products are used by many major companies to promote the sales of their own products or to reinforce their own history and heritage. Frith promotions have been used by Hovis bread, Courage beers, Scots Porage Oats, Colman's mustard, Cadbury's foods, Mellow Birds coffee, Dunhill pipe tobacco, Guinness, and Bulmer's Cider.

Genealogy and Family History

As the interest in family history and roots grows world-wide, more and more people are turning to Frith's photographs of Great Britain for images of the towns, villages and streets where their ancestors lived; and, of course, photographs of the churches and chapels where their ancestors were christened, married and buried are an essential part of every genealogy tree and family album.

Frith Products

All Frith photographs are available Framed or just as Mounted Prints and Posters (size 23 x 16 inches). These may be ordered from the address below. From time to time other products - Address Books, Calendars, Table Mats, etc - are available.

The Internet

Already fifty thousand Frith photographs can be viewed and purchased on the internet through the Frith websites and a myriad of partner sites.

For more detailed information on Frith companies and products, look at these sites:

www.francisfrith.co.uk
www.francisfrith.com
(for North American visitors)

See the complete list of Frith Books at:

www.francisfrith.co.uk

This web site is regularly updated with the latest list of publications from the Frith Book Company. If you wish to buy books relating to another part of the country that your local bookshop does not stock, you may purchase on-line.

For further information, trade, or author enquiries please contact us at the address below:
The Francis Frith Collection, Frith's Barn, Teffont, Salisbury, Wiltshire, England SP3 5QP.
Tel: +44 (0)1722 716 376 Fax: +44 (0)1722 716 881   Email: sales@francisfrith.co.uk

See Frith books on the internet at www.francisfrith.co.uk

FREE MOUNTED PRINT

Mounted Print
Overall size 14 x 11 inches

Fill in and cut out this voucher and return
it with your remittance for £2.25 (to cover postage and handling). Offer valid for delivery to UK addresses only.

Choose any photograph included in this book.
Your SEPIA print will be A4 in size. It will be mounted in a cream mount with a burgundy rule line (overall size 14 x 11 inches).

Order additional Mounted Prints at HALF PRICE (only £7.49 each*)
If you would like to order more Frith prints from this book, possibly as gifts for friends and family, you can buy them at half price (with no additional postage and handling costs).

Have your Mounted Prints framed
For an extra £14.95 per print* you can have your mounted print(s) framed in an elegant polished wood and gilt moulding, overall size 16 x 13 inches (no additional postage and handling required).

---

* IMPORTANT!

These special prices are only available if you order at the same time as you order your free mounted print. You must use the ORIGINAL VOUCHER on this page (no copies permitted). We can only despatch to one address.

Send completed Voucher form to:
The Francis Frith Collection, Frith's Barn, Teffont, Salisbury, Wiltshire SP3 5QP

 *for **FREE** and Reduced Price Frith Prints*

Please do not photocopy this voucher. Only the original is valid, so please fill it in, cut it out and return it to us with your order.

Picture ref no	Page no	Qty	Mounted @ £7.49	Framed + £14.95	Total Cost
		1	Free of charge*	£	£
			£7.49	£	£
			£7.49	£	£
			£7.49	£	£
			£7.49	£	£
			£7.49	£	£

Please allow 28 days for delivery

* Post & handling (UK)	£2.25
Total Order Cost	**£**

Title of this book . . . .

I enclose a cheque/postal order for £ . . . .
made payable to 'The Francis Frith Collection'

OR please debit my Mastercard / Visa / Switch / Amex card
(credit cards please on all overseas orders), details below

Card Number

Issue No (Switch only)   Valid from (Amex/Switch)

Expires   Signature

Name Mr/Mrs/Ms . . . .
Address . . . .
. . . .
. . . .
. . . . Postcode . . . .
Daytime Tel No . . . .
Email . . . .

Valid to 31/12/05

Would you like to find out more about Francis Frith?

We have recently recruited some entertaining speakers who are happy to visit local groups, clubs and societies to give an illustrated talk documenting Frith's travels and photographs. If you are a member of such a group and are interested in hosting a presentation, we would love to hear from you.

Our speakers bring with them a small selection of our local town and county books, together with sample prints. They are happy to take orders. A small proportion of the order value is donated to the group who have hosted the presentation. The talks are therefore an excellent way of fundraising for small groups and societies.

Can you help us with information about any of the Frith photographs in this book?

We are gradually compiling an historical record for each of the photographs in the Frith archive. It is always fascinating to find out the names of the people shown in the pictures, as well as insights into the shops, buildings and other features depicted.

If you recognize anyone in the photographs in this book, or if you have information not already included in the author's caption, do let us know. We would love to hear from you, and will try to publish it in future books or articles.

Our production team

Frith books are produced by a small dedicated team at offices in the converted Grade II listed 18th-century barn at Teffont near Salisbury, illustrated above. Most have worked with the Frith Collection for many years. All have in common one quality: they have a passion for the Frith Collection. The team is constantly expanding, but currently includes:

Jason Buck, John Buck, Ruth Butler, Heather Crisp, David Davies, Isobel Hall, Julian Hight, Peter Horne, James Kinnear, Karen Kinnear, Tina Leary, Stuart Login, Amanda Lowe, David Marsh, Sue Molloy, Kate Rotondetto, Dean Scource, Eliza Sackett, Terence Sackett, Sandra Sampson, Adrian Sanders, Sandra Sanger, Julia Skinner, Claire Tarrier, Lewis Taylor, Shelley Tolcher and Lorraine Tuck.